First Facts®

Animal Rulers

KINGS OF THE JUNGLES

Lisa J. Amstutz

Raintree is an imprint of Capstone Global Library Limited, a company incorporated in England and Wales having its registered office at 264 Banbury Road, Oxford, OX2 7DY – Registered company number: 6695582

www.raintree.co.uk
myorders@raintree.co.uk

Edited by Adrian Vigliano
Designed by Kayla Rossow
Picture research by Kelly Garvin
Production by Kathy McColley
Originated by Captsone Global Library Limited
Printed and bound in India

ISBN 978 1 4747 4860 5 (hardback)
21 20 19 18 17
10 9 8 7 6 5 4 3 2 1

ISBN 978 1 4747 4866 7 (paperback)
22 21 20 19 18
10 9 8 7 6 5 4 3 2 1

British Library Cataloguing in Publication Data
A full catalogue record for this book is available from the British Library.

Acknowledgements
We would like to thank the following for permission to reproduce photographs: Minden Pictures/Piotr Naskrecki, 9; Shutterstock: Aleksey Stemmer, 11, apple2499, cover (top right), glen Gaffney, 15, GUDKOV ANDREY, 21, Horia Bogdan, cover (middle), MarcusVDT, cover (top middle), 19, MattiaATH, 13, neelsky, 7, Signature Message, cover (top left), Sergey Uryadnikov, 17, Smokedsalmon, 5, STILLFX, cover (bottom; artistic elements: Shutterstock: Airin.dizan, Firuz Salamzadeh, leungchopan, Matt Tilghman, mr.Timmi, oorka, Robert Adrian Hillman, Robert Eastman, tbob, Yuri Schmidt

We would like to thank Jackie Gai for her invaluable help in the preparation of this book.

Every effort has been made to contact copyright holders of material reproduced in this book. Any omissions will be rectified in subsequent printings if notice is given to the publisher.

All the internet addresses (URLs) given in this book were valid at the time of going to press. However, due to the dynamic nature of the internet, some addresses may have changed, or sites may have changed or ceased to exist since publication. While the author and publisher regret any inconvenience this may cause readers, no responsibility for any such changes can be accepted by either the author or the publisher.

Contents

Life in the jungle 4

Bengal tiger 6

Goliath birdeater 8

Golden poison dart frog 10

Anaconda 12

Clouded leopard 14

Forest elephant 16

Harpy eagle 18

Orangutan 20

Glossary 22

Find out more 23

Comprehension questions 24

Index 24

Life in the jungle

Deep in the jungle, tigers roar. Birds sing. Insects buzz. Many kinds of animals live in these thick forests. There is plenty to eat in the jungle. But there is always a hungry **predator** lurking nearby. It's eat or be eaten.

predator animal that hunts other animals for food

Bengal tiger

In the dark of night, a Bengal tiger **stalks** its **prey**. Its stripes make the tiger hard to see among the leaves. Its soft paws pad quietly on the jungle floor. With a burst of speed, it pounces. Sharp teeth and claws rip into its prey. Now it can feed its cubs. Bengal tigers live in parts of Asia.

stalk hunt an animal in a quiet, secret way
prey animal that is hunted by other animals for food

Fact! You can hear a tiger's roar up to 3.2 kilometres (2 miles) away!

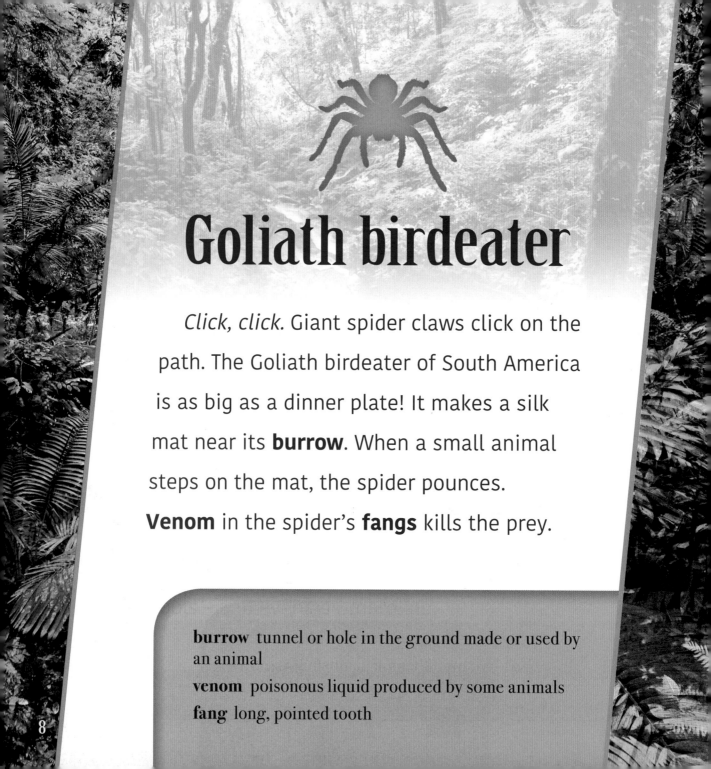

Goliath birdeater

Click, click. Giant spider claws click on the path. The Goliath birdeater of South America is as big as a dinner plate! It makes a silk mat near its **burrow**. When a small animal steps on the mat, the spider pounces. **Venom** in the spider's **fangs** kills the prey.

burrow tunnel or hole in the ground made or used by an animal

venom poisonous liquid produced by some animals

fang long, pointed tooth

Golden poison dart frog

Slurp! A sticky tongue snatches an ant. The tongue belongs to a golden poison dart frog. This cute South American frog is one of the deadliest animals on Earth. Its body holds enough **toxin** to kill 10 people. Its bright colour warns predators not to take a bite. Only one kind of snake can eat golden poison dart frogs. The toxin does not hurt it.

toxin poison

Fact! Golden poison dart frogs don't make their own poison. They collect it from the insects they eat.

Anaconda

Look out! An anaconda lurks in the water. Only its eyes and nostrils stick out of the water. Anacondas eat fish, reptiles and even large mammals. These huge snakes wrap around their prey and squeeze it to death. Then they swallow the prey whole.

Fact! Anacondas live in tropical South America. They can grow up to 9 metres (30 feet) long and weigh up to 204 kilograms (450 pounds).

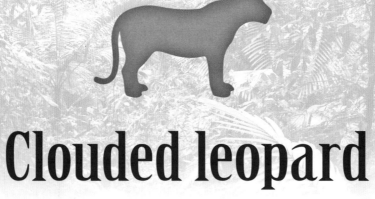

Clouded leopard

Dark spots help **camouflage** a clouded leopard. It is hard to see among the leaves of the Southeast Asian jungle. Its long tail helps it balance on a branch. The leopard leaps down on its prey. It tears flesh with sharp teeth and claws. Leopards eat everything from dung beetles to wild pigs.

camouflage pattern or colour on an animal's skin that makes it blend in with the things around it

Fact! A leopard's spots are called rosettes. They can be round or square, depending on where the animal lives.

Forest elephant

In the jungles of central Africa, a trumpet-like sound rings out. A forest elephant is nearby! Forest elephants are a bit smaller than other elephants. But males still stand more than 2.4 metres (8 feet) tall at the shoulder. Their strong **tusks** push through the thick jungles. They feed on leaves, bark and fruit.

tusk very long, pointed tooth that sticks out when the mouth is closed

Fact! Some elephant sounds are so low that people cannot hear them.

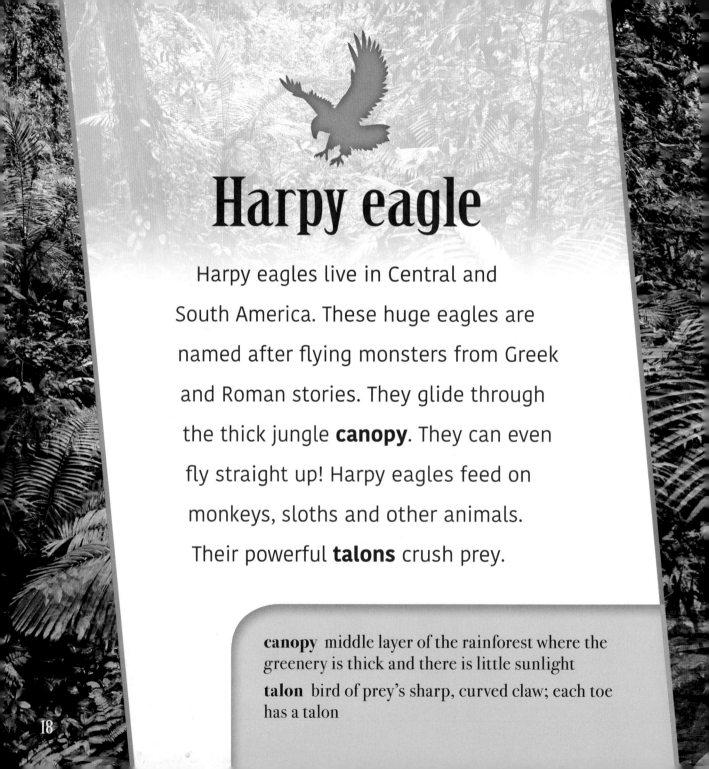

Harpy eagle

Harpy eagles live in Central and South America. These huge eagles are named after flying monsters from Greek and Roman stories. They glide through the thick jungle **canopy**. They can even fly straight up! Harpy eagles feed on monkeys, sloths and other animals. Their powerful **talons** crush prey.

canopy middle layer of the rainforest where the greenery is thick and there is little sunlight

talon bird of prey's sharp, curved claw; each toe has a talon

Fact! A harpy eagle's talons are 12.7 centimetres (5 inches) long. That's longer than a grizzly bear's claws!

Orangutan

On the Asian islands of Borneo and Sumatra, orangutans swing from the trees. Their long, curved fingers and toes are well **adapted** for holding onto branches. Orangutans rarely touch the ground. They live and feed in the trees. These clever animals use sticks and leaves as tools – and even as umbrellas!

adapt change to fit into a new or different environment

Fact! Orangutans are the largest tree-dwelling animals in the world.

Glossary

adapt change to fit into a new or different environment

burrow tunnel or hole in the ground made or used by an animal

camouflage pattern or colour on an animal's skin that makes it blend in with the things around it

canopy middle layer of the rainforest where the greenery is thick and there is little sunlight

fang long, pointed tooth

predator animal that hunts other animals for food

prey animal that is hunted by other animals for food

stalk hunt an animal in a quiet, secret way

talon bird of prey's sharp, curved claw; each toe has a talon

toxin poison

tusk very long, pointed tooth that sticks out when the mouth is closed

venom poisonous liquid made by an animal to kill its prey

Find out more

Books

A Day and Night in the Rainforest (Caroline Arnold's Habitats) Caroline Arnold (Raintree, 2016)

Rainforest, Steve Parker (Priddy Books, 2014)

Rainforests (What Animals Live Here?), M J Knight (Franklin Watts, 2016)

Websites

www.dkfindout.com/uk/animals-and-nature/habitats-and-ecosystems/rainforest-layers
Find out which animals and birds, including the harpy eagle, live in different parts of the rainforest.

gowild.wwf.org.uk/regions/asia-fact-files/bornean-orang-utan
Learn more about the Bornean orangutan.

Comprehension questions

1. How do a Bengal tiger's stripes help it hunt?

2. Where do golden poison dart frogs get their poison?

3. Name two animals that harpy eagles eat.

Index

adaptations 20

fangs 8
fish 12
fruit 16

insects 4, 11

monkeys 18

people 10, 17

sloths 18

talons 18, 19
tools 20
trees 20, 21